The Day
I Fell Down
the Toilet
and
Other Poems

Other poetry books by Steve Turner

Dad, You're Not Funny
The Moon Has Got His Pants On
Don't Take Your Elephant To School
I Was Only Asking

STEVE TURNER

The Day
I Fell Down
the Toilet
and
Other Poems

LION
CHILDREN'S

I WANTED TO BE A LION!

Published by Lion Children's Books
an imprint of
Lion Hudson plc
Wilkinson House, Jordan Hill Road,
Oxford OX2 8DR, England
www.lionhudson.com/lionchildrens

ISBN 978 0 7459 3640 6

First edition 1996
This edition 1997

A catalogue record for this book is available from the British Library

C o n t e n t s

Other Ways of Seeing Things

Who Am I?

Messages to the World

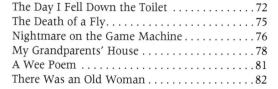

Telling Tales

A Knees-Up With Words

Putting It All Together

THAT POEM'S ABOUT ME.

I Like Words

First Word

The first word I said was 'gaagaa',
Which was shortly followed by 'goo',
And then I stuck them together
To see what a sentence would do.

My Mother was really impressed.
She said, 'Who's a googoo booboo?'
Quick as a flash I responded,
'Oo-gaagaa agoogoo googoo'.

I Like Words

I like words.
Do you like words?
Words aren't hard to find:
Words on walls and words in books,
Words deep in your mind.

Words in jokes
That make you laugh,
Words that seem to smell.
Words that end up inside out,
Words you cannot spell.

Words that fly
And words that crawl,
Words that screech and bump.
Words that glide and words that swing,
Words that bounce and jump.

Words that paint
And words that draw,
Words that make you grin.
Words that make you shake and sweat,
Words that touch your skin.

Words of love
That keep you warm,
Words that make you glad.
Words that hit you, words that hurt,
Words that make you sad.

Words in French
And words in slang,
Words like 'guy' and 'dude',
Words you make up, words you steal,
Words they say are rude.

I like words.
Do you like words?
Words come out and play.
Words are free and words are friends,
Words are great to say.

Language

Dogs bark
Mice squeak
Cats purr
I speak.

Wriggle

Wriggle is a wriggly word.

It runs down from its wrig

Then squiggles on its iggle

And ligs back to its igg.

Wouldn't It Be Funny?

Wouldn't it be funny
if a clock said moo
and a cow when it was
tickled said tick?
Wouldn't it be funny
if a tongue went sniff
and a nose when it was
runny went lick?

Wouldn't it be funny
if bombs went wobble
while a jelly on a
trolley went bang?
Wouldn't it be funny
if a bell went bounce
but a ball if it should
fall went clang?

Wouldn't it be funny
if a crisp went fizz
while the cola in a
bottle went crack?
Wouldn't it be funny
if a fist went sshhh
but a feather when it
fell went whack?

Wouldn't it be funny?
Well, wouldn't it be funny?
Well, wouldn't it be funny like that?

The Naming of the Animals

What would you call this animal, Adam?
He's proud and he prowls and he roars,
He's stronger than anyone else I made
His coat is the colour of straw.

What would you call this animal, Adam?
Her neck stretches up to the trees,
She has four legs as skinny as sticks
And four very knobbly knees.

What would you call this animal, Adam,
With a tube instead of a nose?
His ears are like clothes on a washing line
And he hurrumphs wherever he goes.

What would you call this animal, Adam?
Her skin is as tough as old rope,
A horn sticks up on the end of her nose
And mud is her favourite soap.

What would you call this animal, Adam?
He swoops from the sky for his lunch,
He knits his own house from branches and leaves
And swallows a mouse with a crunch.

What would you call this person, Adam?
I want her to be your best friend.
Make sure you love her with all of your heart
And stay by her side 'til the end.

WHY WASN'T I
IN THIS POEM!

What Am I?

This bow is made of sunshine
This bow is made of rain
This bow is many-coloured
This bow says not again.

Words I Like

Billowing, seaboard, ocean, pearl,
Estuary, shale, maroon;
Harlequin, runnel, ripple, swirl,
Labyrinth, lash, lagoon.

Razorbill, cygnet, songbird, kite,
Cormorant, crag, ravine;
Flickering, sun-burst, dappled, flight,
Fiery, dew, serene.

Asteroid, nova, star-dust, moon,
Galaxy, zone, eclipse;
Dynamo, pulsar, planet, rune,
Satellite, spangle, lips.

Boulevard, freeway, turnpike, cruise,
Chevrolet, fin, pavanne;
Tomahawk, firecrest, fantail, fuse,
Saskatchewan, Sioux, Cheyenne.

Tenderness, sweetheart, cherish, miss,
Paramour, fond, befriend;
Affection, cosy, cuddle, kiss,
Family, love, the end.

Rhythm and Rhyme

Heartbeat

I can hear my heart beat –
Lying in my bed,
I can feel the blood rush
Pounding in my head,
Beating like a bass drum
In an empty room,
I can hear my heart beat
Boom-de, boom-de, boom.

Seasons

Spring, summer, autumn, winter
Every year the same –
Round and round the seasons go
Like a party game.
Spin the leaves from green to brown
Spin them on to gold,
Turn the weather up to hot
Turn it down to cold.
Chase the clouds across the sky
Paint a yellow sun,
Then the rain comes tumbling down
Spoiling all our fun.

Spring, summer, autumn, winter
Every year the same –
Round and round the seasons go
Like a party game.

Drip Drip Drip

Drip drip drip
Goes the tap tap tap
And tap tap tap
Goes the twig twig twig
And rustle rustle rustle
Goes the wind wind wind
And shudder shudder shudder
Goes the pipe pipe pipe
And creak creak creak
Goes the floor floor floor
And mumble mumble mumble
Goes the telly next door.

Rustle, shudder, tap and drip
Rumble, mumble, creak and snore
How can children sleep at night
When the house begins to roar?

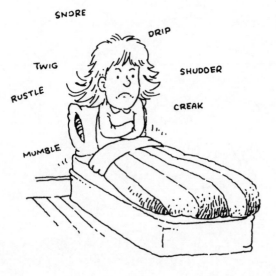

Breathing

I'm very good at breathing,
I do it every day,
I didn't have to learn it,
For I was born that way.

Into the world I bounded,
At 15 breaths per min,
(That's 15 puffing out bits
And 15 sniffing in).

I don't know how I do it,
I've never had to think.
How do I make my heart beat?
Who taught me how to blink?

I'm very good at breathing,
I do it slow and deep,
I do it fast and shallow,
I do it in my sleep.

I do it when I'm running,
Or standing on my head,
And when they think I've finished,
I'll do it when I'm dead!

Jack and Jill

Jack and Jill went up the hill.
What's so good about that?
Jack fell down and broke his crown,
The careless, clumsy brat.

Boring Boring Boring

There's nothing left for me to do
I'm bored with them
I'm bored with you
I'm bored with staying in my room
I'm bored with going shopping too
I'm bored with sleep
I'm bored in bed
I'm bored with all the food I'm fed
I'm bored out of my boring head
I feel as if I'm boring dead.
I'm bored with clouds
I'm bored with rain
I'm bored with my computer game
I'm bored that everything's the same
I'm bored with being bored again.
I'm bored with writing boring rhymes
About my boring boring times
And so I'll finish...

InterCity Train

We're on the InterCity train
Rolling along the tracks again
Calling at A and B and C
Serving coffee and cakes and tea
Rattling past the backs of houses
Lines of socks and shirts and trousers
Football nets and cricketing creases
Cars and bikes all left in pieces.

Through the curtains, the lighted halls
Posters hanging from bedroom walls
Silhouette heads through frosted glass
Spades and barrows in jungle grass
Gaggles of geese and flocks of birds
Bridges and walls with painted words
Towering chimneys belching clouds
Summery parks with swarming crowds.

Whistling past the names of places
Platforms left as empty spaces
Banks of bushes to left and right
Tunnelling dark and into light
Smouldering leaves on garden fires
Miles and miles of telegraph wires
Lights that change from orange to red
Cows and sheep that need to be fed.

We're on the InterCity Train
Rolling along the tracks again
Calling at A and B and C
Serving coffee and cakes and tea
Drawing near our destination
Meeting friends outside the station
Pack your bags and close your cases
It's such fun to go to places.

Like This... Like That

As Good As This

As right as rain
As wrong as no
As up as sky
As fast as go.

As tough as nails
As soft as soap
As short as shoes
As long as rope.

As nice as pie
As good as gold
As smooth as new
As rough as old.

As then as was
As now as is
As bad as that
As good as this.

My Love is Like a Red Red Rose

My love is like a red red rose
Her beauty makes you stare,
She stands alone near garden lawns
While bees hum in her hair.

My love is like a red red rose
Her body's green and thin,
And when I try to squeeze her waist
She sticks her prickles in.

My love is like a red red rose
She's wilting by the hour,
It makes no sense to fall in love
With someone like a flower.

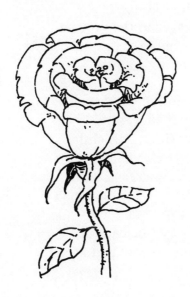

What Have You Done to the Wind?

What have you done to the wind, now,
And why is it moaning outside?
Why is it screaming through keyholes
And why is it trying to hide?

Why is it banging the gate shut
And causing the gutter to leak?
Why is it howling like hound dogs
Which haven't been fed for a week?

What have you done to the wind, now,
And why is it drunk in the street?
Why is it tossing our tiles down
And trampling our plants with its feet?

Why is it climbing the tree-tops
While shaking the leaves to the ground?
Why is it hurling our bin-lids
And making a frightening sound?

What have you done to the wind, now,
To make it so terribly mad?
Did you slash the air with a golf club
Or whisper a word that was bad?

Did you stab the breeze with your finger
Or dice it to bits with your car?
With weather you have to be careful,
For wind always knows where you are.

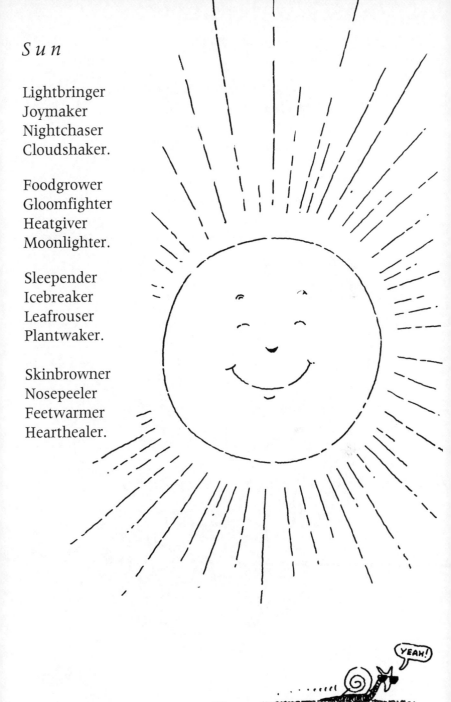

Sun

Lightbringer
Joymaker
Nightchaser
Cloudshaker.

Foodgrower
Gloomfighter
Heatgiver
Moonlighter.

Sleepender
Icebreaker
Leafrouser
Plantwaker.

Skinbrowner
Nosepeeler
Feetwarmer
Hearthealer.

YEAH!

Butterflies

I've got butterflies in my stomach,
And elephants in my head,
My heart's turned into a kangaroo.
Why can't they go to bed?

It's Raining Cats and Dogs

It's raining cats and dogs –
The sky is growing dark,
Instead of pitter-patter
It's splatter, yowl and bark.

Bulldogs bounce on bonnets,
Alsatians hang in trees,
Poodles land on policemen
And bring them to their knees.

Tabby cats come squealing
Like rockets overhead,
Siamese look worried
At pavements turning red.

It's raining cats and dogs,
Although it shouldn't oughta.
Next time I pray for rain,
I'll add that I mean water.

Sitting by a Summer Pool

Sitting by a summer pool
You see no swanky suits,
No overcoats or trousers,
No Doctor Martens boots.

No one knows who's rich or poor
Or who drives what year's car;
When skin is all you have to wear
You are just what you are.

NO DIVING
NO JUMPING
NO SPLASHING
NO SWIMMING
NO NOTHING

Managers of city banks
Who like their suits well pressed,
Show skin which was all crumpled up
Beneath their clean white vests.

Bellies which were proudly slapped
While drinking at The Grapes,
Are bulging like the mammoth fronts
Of hairy jungle apes.

Girls who think they're movie stars
Don't look the stuff of dreams,
When hair is flat and dripping wet
And face is washed of creams.

Tough kids lose their shoulder pads,
Their belts and buckles, too;
It's hard to look a thug in trunks
When ribs are showing through.

Policemen out of uniform
And choir boys without smocks,
Punks without their safety pins
And girl guides without socks.

Pop stars without microphones
And waiters without tips,
Nuns without their habits on
And jockeys without whips.

Queens without their studded crowns
And bakers without buns,
Tramps without their plastic bags
And soldiers without guns.

Ballet dancers without tights
And teachers without school,
Everyone is what they are
Beside the summer pool.

Who Was I Before I Was Born?

You were a song
that had yet to be sung,
You were a word
on the tip of a tongue,
You were a plan
chalked up on a board
You were a gleam
in the eye of the Lord.

Memory and Magic

I Like the World

I like the world
The world is good
World of water
World of wood
World of feather
World of bone
World of mountain
World of stone.

World of fibre
World of spark
World of sunshine
World of dark
World of raindrop
World of dew
World of me
and
World of you.

The Jumping Game

We jump the rope
We jump in line
We jump up high
We jump in time
We jump for luck
We jump again
We jump along
The jumping game.

We jump in ones
We jump in twos
We jump the lights
We jump the queues
We jump for joy
We jump again
We jump along
The jumping game.

We jump and fall
We jump and learn
We jump and twist
We jump and turn
We jump for kicks
We jump again
We jump along
The jumping game.

We jump for gold
We jump for free
We jump from A
We jump to B
We jump for fun
We jump again
We jump along
The jumping game.

Old Swear Word

An old swear word has been found
That few have ever heard,
Hidden in a box it was
A very naughty word.

On scraps of grubby paper
In marks of ancient ink,
A secret from another age
Returns to cause a stink.

They say it's so explosive
The army has been called,
A policeman who just looked in
Went absolutely bald.

If it was ever spoken
All switchboards would be jammed,
The government would argue
That such things should be banned.

But maybe they should save it
In case of World War Three,
A cheap and secret weapon
To beat the enemy.

If nuclear strikes were threatened
They'd open up the box,
And shout the horrid word out
Then everything would stop.

In a country far away
A million knees would knock,
As members of the public
Went reeling from the shock.

Faces would go hot and cold
And turn to greys and reds,
Eyes would open wide as doors
And pop from people's heads.

Dying of embarrassment
The enemy would flip,
For funny things can happen
When naughty words just slip.

Sleepy Time

Bless my eyes
And bless my head,
Bless my dreams
Upon this bed.

Spell

By the mound of the moon
And the spikes in the stars
Bring down my sleep onto me.

By circles of Saturn
And the mountains of Mars
Bring down my sleep onto me.

By the deep of the dark
And the silence of streams
Bring down my sleep onto me.

By the hoot of the owl
And the dungeon of dreams
Bring down my sleep onto me.

By the sound of my spell
And the breath on my bed
Bring down my sleep onto me.

In the Beginning

God said WORLD
and the world spun round,
God said LIGHT
and the light beamed down,
God said LAND
and the sea rolled back,
God said NIGHT
and the sky went black.

God said LEAF
and the shoot pushed through,
God said FIN
and the first fish grew,
God said BEAK
and the big bird soared,
God said FUR
and the jungle roared.

God said SKIN
and the man breathed air,
God said BONE
and the girl stood there,
God said GOOD
and the world was great,
God said REST
and they all slept late.

Standing On My Head

One times two is two,
Two times two is four.
Maths is very hard,
Arithmetic's a bore.
Three times two is six,
Four times two is eight,
Algebra is dumb,
Geometry I hate.
Five times two is three,
Six times two is red.
I can do my tables
Standing on my head.

Other Ways
of Seeing Things

Upside Down

When I'm upside down
It's a very funny feeling,
There are bushes and trees
Growing out of the ceiling,
While the sky pours into
A puddle on the ground,
It's a very funny feeling
When I'm upside down.

G h o s t s

I'd like to be a ghost I would,
To be a ghost is cool.
For ghosts don't have to go to work
And ghosts don't go to school.

A ghost can stay up late at night
(In fact they always do),
And ghosts get rooms all to themselves
By simply shouting, 'whoooooooooooooooo!'

I Am the Sea

I wrestle and roll
I lap and I lick
I turn into foam
and make people sick.

I wear away rock
I guzzle up sand
I swallow up ships
and creep over land.

I am the sea
I am the sea
Listen to me
Listen to me.

I float up as clouds
I fall down as rain
I soak through the earth
then come back again.

I glide over pebbles
I gurgle in streams
Run down in rivers
and open your dreams.

I am the sea
I am the sea
Listen to me
Listen to me.

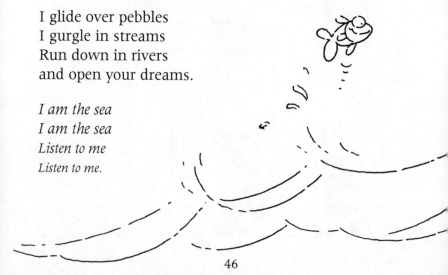

I once was a mist
I once was the sky
I once was a tear
Which filled up your eye.

I stung you with salt
I made your wood rot
I've been making waves
Ever since the year dot.

I am the sea
I am the sea
Listen to me
Listen to me.

TV Dinner

*(One day Nathan asked, 'Dad, why can't we
watch sandwiches and eat televisions?')*

I suppose you could watch a sandwich
If you possessed a permanent stare;
You could sit yourself in a sofa
And prop a large slice on a chair.

But bread is exceedingly boring
It comes only in white or in brown,
You can't switch from channel to channel
And none of it makes any sound.

What is there to see on a sandwich?
There's nothing until it gets old,
Then you can watch corners curling
And the growth of hairy green mould.

I suppose you could eat a TV
But not for your breakfast or lunch;
Maybe as a snack in the evening –
A little light something to crunch.

I'd suggest you serve it in portions
(It's too much to swallow, of course),
The valves could be mixed in with coleslaw,
The wires could be cooked in a sauce.

The screen could be ground to a powder
For sprinkling on carrots or beans,
The plastic could melt to a syrup
For pouring all over ice-cream.

You could eat your telly while watching
A sandwich preserved in a jar;
But I'd say, when all is considered,
It's best to leave things as they are.

The Vegetables Strike Back

'I don't like vegetables at all!'
Said Nathan one evening at tea.
But what the young lad didn't know
Was that vegetables hear and see.

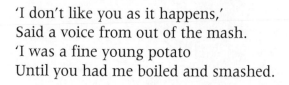

'I don't like you as it happens,'
Said a voice from out of the mash.
'I was a fine young potato
Until you had me boiled and smashed.

'Just think how you'd like to be skinned,
Or baked alive in your jacket.
How would you feel to be crumbled up,
Then stuffed inside of a packet?

'You tear peas out of their houses
And drag them away from their mums.
You stick knives into baby beans
And forks into cucumber's bums.

'You fatten a lettuce or cabbage,
Then cut off its head with a knife.
Drive runner beans up bamboo poles
In order to choke them of life.

'I've had good friends who've been frozen,
Or left in a shed to shrink up.
Some were burned up in an oven
And some became soup in a cup.

'You spread fear round every garden
When you come to kill and destroy,
Stabbing and cutting and slicing
With your latest gardening toy.

'You say you don't like vegetables,
Well, we don't like vandals like you,
Who put us in bags and boxes,
Then drown us in steaming hot stew.'

The mouth of the boy fell open,
His fork hovered high in the air.
His knife was all ready to cut,
But now did he dare? Did he dare?

The Final Straw

I hit my sister.
My dad got mad.

Dad said, 'Get right in your bed. Now.'
So I did. I got right in.
I slit open the mattress
With a sharpened blade
and I slid right in.
It was a tight fit
between those springs.

So Dad said, 'That's destructive.
Stay in your room. And don't you dare come out.'
So I did.
Monday, Tuesday, Wednesday,
Thursday, Friday.
I stayed in my room.
I got lonely. And hungry.

So Dad said, 'Come down here
and eat some food.
Now you eat everything. You hear?'
So I did.
I ate the egg, the chips and the beans.
The plate, the knife, the fork.
The table.

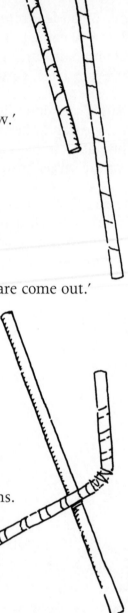

So Dad said, 'You've gone too far.
You make me sick to death.'
So I picked up the 'phone.
I called an ambulance.
'Come quickly. My dad's sick...
How sick? Sick to death.'
The sound of sirens
soon filled the street.
They carried Dad off on a stretcher.
They had to strap him down
to stop him struggling.

So Dad said, 'That's the final straw!'
(But it wasn't.
There was a spare one
stuck onto a carton of fruit juice
in the fridge.)

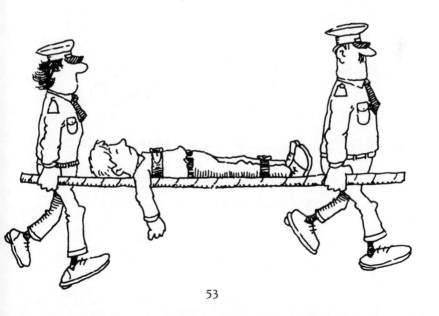

I'll Run Away From Home

I'll run away from home, I will,
I'll run away from home,
I'll disappear one afternoon
Then call you on the phone.

You'll scream and shout, you'll weep and wail,
You'll cry, 'What have we done?'
And then I'll say, 'I'm right next door.
It's just a bit of fun!'

I'll vanish without trace, I will,
I'll lose myself at sea,
And then you'll wish you hadn't been
So beastly bad to me.

You'll scream and shout, you'll weep and wail,
Throw flowers from a ship,
And then I'll swim by, shouting out,
'Who's coming for a dip?'

You'll find me dead in bed, you will,
You'll find me dead in bed,
And then you'll feel so bad about
The nasty things you said.

You'll cry and shout, you'll weep and wail,
You'll gasp and scream and choke
And then I'll jump up laughing loud,
'Well, can't you take a joke?'

Who Am I?

The Olden Days

What was it like in the olden days, Dad,
In the days when you were a boy?
Did you wash your hands with water and soap?
Did you have a favourite toy?

Did you wear your blazer and cap to school?
Did your trousers come down to your knees?
Did teachers hit you with slippers and sticks?
Did you all say 'thank you' and 'please'?

What was it like in the olden days, Mum,
In the days when you were like me?
Did you have such things as buses and cars?
Did the water still fill the sea?

Did the moon shine down from the same dark sky?
Did the stars still twinkle at night?
Did you have such colours as yellow and red?
Or was everything just black and white?

God Is Still
Making Up Numbers

1	2	3	4	5	6	7	8	9	10	11	12	13
14	15	16	17	18	19	20	21	22	23	24	25	26
27	28	29	30	31	32	33	34	35	36	37	38	39
40	41	42	43	44	45	46	47	48	49	50	51	52
53	54	55	56	57	58	59	60	61	62	63	64	65
66	67	68	69	70	71	72	73	74	75	76	77	78
79	80	81	82	83	84	85	86	87	88	89	90	91
92	93	94	95	96	97	98	99	100	101	102	103	
104	105	106	107	. . . .								

God is still making up numbers
For numbers just go on and on...
Just when God thinks he has finished
God knows he can always add 1.

Who Made the World?

Who was it who made the world, Sir?
A bang brought creation about.
Who set off the explosion, Sir?
I don't know. They're still finding out.

Did this big bang make you deaf, Sir?
It happened a long time ago.
How do you know it happened, Sir?
A man in a book told me so.

Who was the man in the book, Sir?
A man who looked up in the sky.
How do you know that he knew, Sir?
Because I believe him, that's why.

Who was it made me and you, Sir?
A creature crept out of the sea.
Who was it made the creature, Sir?
The creature just happened to be.

Why did it creep from the sea, Sir?
It thought it was time for a change.
How did it grow arms and legs, Sir?
I know, it sounds awfully strange.

Where do we go when we die, Sir?
Don't know, but I'm sure that it's great.
Who was it made the place great, Sir?
No talking now children, it's late.

Hard to Please

I don't like stings from wasps or bees
I don't like friends to see my knees
I don't like war, don't like disease
That's why they call me hard to please.

I don't like milk that smells like cheese
I don't like coughs that start to wheeze
I don't like spots you have to squeeze
That's why they call me hard to please.

I don't like baths that start to freeze
I don't like friends who taunt and tease
I don't like last week's mushy peas
That's why they call me hard to please.

It Wasn't Me

It wasn't me, my cup just fell,
The plate jumped on the floor,
The window cracked all by itself
And then it slammed the door.

I didn't punch, my hand just slipped
And curled into a fist.
He happened to come walking by,
I happened not to miss.

It wasn't me who talked in class,
I didn't steal that pen,
If someone says they saw me cheat
They've got it wrong again.

It wasn't me, it's not my fault!
Why do I get the blame?
The naughty child who does these things
Has pinched my face and name.

My Dad

My dad's bigger than your dad.
My dad's as tall as the moon,
as strong as the wind,
as wide as the sky.
You should see my dad!
He's got stars in his fists.
He bends rainbows on his knee.
When he breathes, clouds move.

He's good is my dad.
You can't scare him with the dark.
You can't scare him with guns or sticks.
He makes bullies say sorry
just by staring.
Big green monsters
fall asleep on his lap.
Ghosts start haunting each other.

My dad's been everywhere
but he says he likes the world.
Earth people are fun he says.
My dad knows more than teacher.
He knows everything.
He knows what you're thinking,
even when you try to trick him
by thinking something else.
If you tell a lie
my dad says he can tell
by the look on your face.

My dad's the best dad ever.
I say I love him
a million times a million
times a million times a million trillion.
My dad says he loves me
a billion trillion times more than that.

My dad likes to love.
My dad made the world.

I Can't Sit Still

I can do a somersault
and I can count to ten,
I can walk a thousand miles
and then walk back again,
I can climb up Everest
Like walking up a hill,
I can fold my clothes up neat
but me, I can't sit still.

I can beat the bully brats
With fine karate chops,
I can sleep without a light
And go alone to shops,
I can bounce on trampolines
Walk on the window-sill,
I can say my prayers at night
But me, I can't sit still.

I can jump like kangaroos
and I can swim like fish,
I can swing from chandeliers
and dive into a dish,
I can beat the champions
one hundred goals to nil,
I can tie my shoelaces
But me, I can't sit still.

Teacher calls me 'wrigglebum'
My mum calls me a 'pest',
I think they want to help me
To settle down and rest,
I try to cross my ankles
and do the proper drill,
I can even fold my arms,
But me, I can't sit still.

I'M GOOD
AT KEEPING
STILL.

Who's a Lovely Girl?

Well, who's a lovely girl then?
(Not me, you stupid bat.)
And who's got shiny hair then?
(You'd think I was the cat.)

You're so much like your mummy.
(I think I'm just like me.)
With little bits of grandma.
(I have to disagree.)

And, wow, you have grown taller!
(That's what we humans do.)
And who's a clever girl then?
(Obviously not you.)

Messages to the World

Who Made a Mess?

Who made a mess of the planet
And what's that bad smell in the breeze?
Who punched a hole in the ozone
And who took an axe to my trees?

Who sprayed the garden with poison
While trying to scare off a fly?
Who streaked the water with oil slicks
And who let my fish choke and die?

Who tossed that junk in the river
And who stained the fresh air with fumes?
Who tore the fields with a digger
And who blocked my favourite views?

Who's going to tidy up later
And who's going to find what you've lost?
Who's going to say that they're sorry
And who's going to carry the cost?

All We Need

Food in our bellies
Hats on our heads
Water to quench us
Sheets on our beds.

Teachers to teach us
Shoes on our feet
Trousers and T-shirts
Shelter and heat.

Someone to love us
Someone to love
Hope for the future
Light from above.

Television News

While we take burgers, cokes and fries
The TV tells of hate and lies
Shows death beneath bright foreign skies
Can someone pass the salt?

The ground is parched, the river dies
The Red Cross camp has no supplies
The cold night air is cut with cries
Which ice-cream have you bought?

With bones stuck out like blunted knives
And bellies swollen twice the size
The people cling to fading lives
Who's washing up tonight?

We see their pain in bulging eyes
And faces gaunt and thick with flies
The camera zooms as someone dies
What's on the other side?

I Know the Santa

I know the Santa whose feet I heard creep
I know the sandman who sends me to sleep
I know the reindeer who walks on my roof
I know the fairy who found my front tooth.

I know the green elf who makes all my toys
I know the monster who makes all that noise
I know the birdie who sees what I do
I know them all, and they all look like you.

More Sweets

*('How can the world be made a better place?' I asked
Lianne. She thought the answer was more sweets.)*

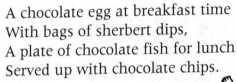

The world would be a better place
If we could have more sweets –
More bubble gum and candy sticks,
More Smarties, Mars and Treats.

A chocolate egg at breakfast time
With bags of sherbert dips,
A plate of chocolate fish for lunch
Served up with chocolate chips.

Instead of getting milk at school
We'd all drink Coke and Sprite,
And sitting at our classroom desks
We'd eat just what we liked.

Then home for tea of fudge and flake
and bowls of soft ice-cream,
A toffee bar we'd take to bed
To chew on while we dream.

The world would be a better place
If we could have more sweets –
There'd be no time for hate and war
If all we did was eat.

Telling Tales

Inside My Head

Inside my head there's a forest,
A castle, a cottage, a king,
A rose, a thorn, some golden hair,
A turret, a tower, a ring.

A horse, a prince, a secret word,
A giant, a gaol, a pond,
A witch, a snake, a bubbling pot,
A wizard, a warlock, a wand.

Inside my head there's an ocean,
A parrot, a pirate, a gull,
A cave, a sword, a silver coin,
A princess, an island, a skull.

A ghost, a ghoul, a creaking stair,
A shadow, a shudder, a shout,
A flame, a grave, a swirling mist,
A rainbow, an angel, a cloud.

Inside my head there's a country
Of mountains and valleys and streams,
It all comes alive when I listen
To stories, to poems, to dreams.

What I Did Last Night

You'll never guess what I did last night –
I gave an old ghost a terrible fright,
I tickled his bones and pulled his chains
Then kicked him back down the stairway again.

You'll never guess what I did last night –
I gave a monster a monstrous bite,
I stuck a hot flame right up her nose
Then jumped up and down on each of her toes.

You'll never guess what I did last night –
Me and a robot got into a fight,
I pulled all its plugs and snipped its wires,
Bent it to bits with a hammer and pliers.

You'll never guess what I did last night –
I caught an old witch and painted her white,
I battered her hat and broke her broom
Then locked her away in the smallest room.

You'll never guess what I did last night –
I woke from a dream and turned on the light.

The Day I Fell Down the Toilet

The day I fell down the toilet
Is a day I'll never forget,
One moment I was in comfort
The next I was helpless and wet.

My feet tipped up to the ceiling
My body collapsed in the bowl,
In haste I grabbed at the handle
And found myself flushed down a hole.

One wave goodbye to the bathroom
And I was lost in the sewer,
Travelling tunnels and caverns
On a raft made out of manure.

Then came the washing-up water
With bits of spaghetti and peas,
The filth from a local factory
And an undiscovered disease.

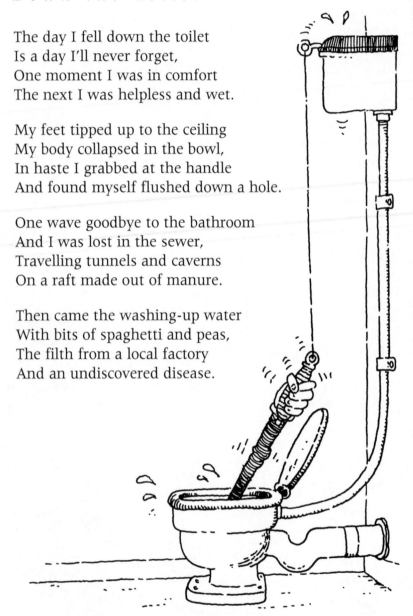

Drifting along in the darkness,
There was nothing to do but wait.
What would I say to my mum now?
What was it that made me so late?

Suddenly it was all over,
From the end of a pipe I shot
Into a part of the ocean
Where the rubbish was sent to rot.

Glad to escape from the tunnel
To leave all pollution behind,
I found a nice spot on the beach
Then started to bathe and unwind.

But bad things began to pursue me
They stuck to my feet and my hand,
Wreckage was surfing the wave tops
And oil lay around on the sand.

I figured the sewer was safer
For no one said sewers were clean,
I found the pipe that I came from.
And waded my way back upstream.

When I got home I was shattered,
I was filthy, ragged and wet,
Rattling the bathroom door was Dad
Saying, 'You off that toilet yet?'

The Death of a Fly

Fly see saucer
Fly fly down
Me see fly fly
Fly walk 'round.

Fly take big sip
Me take spoon
Fly look wrong way
Spoon go boom.

Cup go wobble
Tea go splat
Fly get big fright
Fly get flat.

Fly not fly now
Fly not sip
Fly just flied on
Final trip.

Nightmare on the Game Machine

My little boy is perfect
He really is a dream
That is until he gets on
His video machine.

Then he becomes a monster
His face turns shades of red
I'm sure I saw a tail shake
And horns grow from his head.

'I've just got killed,' he bellows
(Although he looks all right)
He bangs down on the buttons
To start another fight.

The creatures leap like crazy
While bleepers bleep and curse
He pushes all the right things
The game gets worse and worse.

'I'm at the highest level'
'I need just one more star'
'It took me months to get here'
'I've never been so far'.

Their shooting is appalling
They all begin to drop
He presses JUMP, they lie down
He presses GO, they stop.

He screams and cries with anger
Then crumples on the floor
'I've had enough,' he slobbers
'I can't play any more.'

Fire shoots from his nose and mouth
And melts the TV screen
Teeth cut through the plugs and wires
Then crush the game machine.

The video's defeated
A broken washed-up toy
The monster has departed
We welcome back our boy.

My little boy is perfect
He really is a dream
That is until he gets on
His video machine.

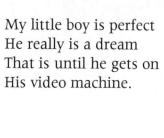

My Grandparents' House

When I was a boy my grandparents lived
In a house that was centuries old,
The staircases creaked
The door-hinges squeaked
And the hallways were icily cold.

One wintry night, the story is told,
The family had all gone to bed
When each heard the fall
Of feet in the hall
Growing louder and then going dead.

Somebody it seemed was standing right there
And would next turn a knob on a door
'Who's there?' a voice said
From out of a bed,
But no footsteps were heard any more.

When morning arrived and breakfast was served
They talked over cereal and toast
'I heard you last night!'
'You gave me a fright!'
'I expected to meet with a ghost!'

'But it wasn't me!' said everyone there
Their voices now wavering with fear.
'Then, who made the noise?'
Asked one of the boys
But no one had any idea.

Then grandfather spoke of the lady in grey
I perhaps should have told you before.
She comes and she goes
But nobody knows
Why she's restless or what she looks for.

'The stairs in this house came from the ruins
Of a castle which once held a queen
Who was sentenced to death
And took her last breath
As she walked down the steps you've just seen.

'I've heard the footsteps, the creaking of boards,
The rustle of fine linen and lace
But never have seen
The robes of the queen
Or the haunted grey look of her face.'

When I was a boy my grandparents lived
In a house that was centuries old
The staircases creaked
The door-hinges squeaked
And the hallways were icily cold.

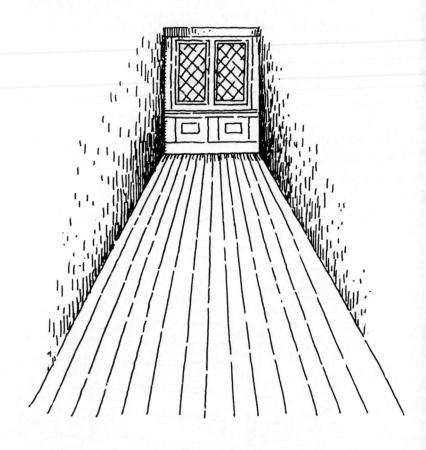

A Wee Poem

Please don't be slow taking me home
I need to go for a wee.
I try to think of something else
But a wee just wants to wee.

Oh no, it's Mr Barnstaple
Taking his dog for a walk.
Please pretend he's invisible
He'll only stop for a talk.

Now Barnstaple has spotted you
He was just about to call.
He's got all the time in the world
And I've got no time at all.

I mustn't think of waterfalls
Or taps or bubbling streams,
I have to cross my legs and think
Of mashed potatoes and greens.

At last the man he walks away
And I think I'm home and dry
I want to bounce from here to there
With one big leap through the sky.

But suddenly my worries go
There's nothing more I can do –
My heart is warm and so's my leg
And there's squelching in my shoe.

There Was an Old Woman

There was an old woman
Who lived in a shoe.
The council decided
It just wouldn't do.
They blocked up the lace holes,
They stuffed it with socks,
Then moved all the children
To a new cardboard box.

A Knees-Up With Words

The Ding-Dong Song

A bell on a bus has a ding
Where a bell on a rope has a dong.
A bicycle bell has a prrring
But a gong, as you know, has a bong.
  A gong, as you know, has a bong.

DING! DONG! PRRIING! CLANG! PING

A bell on a door has a ping
And a bell on a clock has a clang.
A telephone bell doesn't ring
Yet it purrs and we say that it rang.
  It purrs and we say that it rang.

BONG PURRS CLONG ting!

A bell in a shop has a ting
And a bell on a cow has a clong.
There is nothing to say about this
But I thought you might like this wee song.
  I thought you might like this wee song.

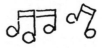

A Knees-Up With Words

Words can look so serious
Dressed up in black on white,
Making sure their 'p's and 'q's
Are absolutely right.

Sitting there in pretty rows
Like soldiers on parade,
Not trespassing in margins
Nor falling off the page.

But words they like to party
They like to dance and pun,
To shake their punctuation
In a carnival of fun.

Adjectives can tightrope walk,
Unfriendly words can mix,
Nouns can bounce on trampolines,
While verbs play cunning tricks.

Full stops like to roll around
And not lie at the end.
Question marks get up and stretch,
While exclamations bend.

CAPITALS can shrink in size
While smaller words get BIG.
Sentences can do the twist
And paragraphs can jig.

Words can look so serious
Dressed up in black on white,
They need to have a party,
So take them out tonight.

Punch-Line

A zebra rolling down a hill.
Pardon?
A zebra rolling down a hill.
What do you mean?
What goes black white black white black?
Oh, I see. Your joke's back to front.
Silly me. I got dressed in the dark.

Week

moanday
BLUESDAY
WHINESDAY
BLURSDAY
FLY D A Y
SPLATTERDAY
FUNDAY

Tomorrow

Tomorrow's never there.
It always runs away.
Every time I catch it
It says it's called Today.

Bottoms

Who called a bottom a bottom?
It's not at the bottom at all.
Bottoms are not where our feet are
So bottoms are not what they're called.

I'd call a bottom a middle
It's not at the bottom or top
It's just at the back of the front
The bit where our legs start to stop.

Now feet, they *are* at the bottom
The bottom of me and of you
But think of the problems we'd have
If bottoms were things wearing shoes.

''Scuse me, you stood on my bottom'
'I must rest my bottoms awhile'
Football would hardly be mentioned
As bottomball came into style.

All day we'd stand on our bottoms
Or sit on our middles at school
Someone would stick a bottom out
And cause us to stumble and fall.

But feet don't want to be bottoms
They think they are silly and thick
Which is why whenever they meet
The foot gives the bottom a kick.

Bugler Bill

Have you heard about Bugler Bill
Who armed with his bugle and voice
Climbs over garden fences and walls
To play you the tune of your choice?

Well, he used to be Burglar Bill
Before his big musical break
His criminal life was brought to a halt
By a stupid spelling mistake.

Putting It All Together

Strings and Things

Don't throw out that cardboard
I want that piece of string
Save all silver paper
Don't throw away a thing.

Peel the stamps off letters
Collect the cards from tea
Never squash an empty box
Just keep them all for me.

Styrofoam and plastic
Unusual shapes of stone
Coins found in the garden
Odd bits of broken bone.

Keys that don't fit keyholes
And pens that have no ink
Bottles without fluid
And cans dried up of drink.

I'm the friend of objects
That others think are junk
I play with them for days
(Then lose them in my bunk).

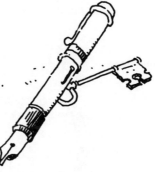

The Worst School
in the World

It's the worst school in the world
And it starts at six every day
You're not allowed to talk to friends
Or go outside to play.

There's barbed wire on the fences
An army patrol at the gate
You get sent to prison for running
Beheaded for turning up late.

Rottweilers stand in as prefects
Patrolling the cloakrooms in pairs
Keeping an eye on the toilets
And lying in wait on the stairs.

The head is a Sumo wrestler
With a beard and very bad breath
Who wears jackboots under her dress
And has knuckles tattooed with DEATH.

The teachers all look like extras
From films they won't show on TV
Like 'Even Worse Nightmare on Elm Street'
And 'Frankenstein Comes Home To Tea'.

Their shouts can rattle a desk lid
And their looks can strip paint off wood
Yes, it may seem hard at the time
But the exam results are good.

Lists

I'm great at writing lists, I am,
Of things that I must do.
I'm great at writing number one
Then writing number two.

I'm great at putting 'Must do this!'
With exclamation marks:
Must tidy bedroom up today!!
Must walk dog in the park!!

Must do my homework after school!!
(I'll write that on my wrist.)
Must save more cash for holidays!!
Must start another list.

I never get these jobs all done,
I don't do as I should;
It's just that when I write a list
It makes me feel so good.

Snail

A snail cannot run,
A snail cannot race,
A snail only slides
At a snail-like pace.

Round in a circle,
Along in a line,
A snail lays a trail
Of a silvery slime.

A snail never swims,
A snail never walks,
A snail has its eyes
On the top of two stalks.

Round in a ziggle,
Along in a zag,
A snail has a house
In a shell on its back.

A snail's never in,
A snail's never out,
A snail is around
And around and about.

Round in a squiggle,
Along in a squirl,
A snail lays a trail
In a small, small world.

SMALL, BUT
NOT FORGOTTEN!

Fireworks

Fire sticks shoot through billowing black,
Ice-creamy sparkles tumble and crack,
Red carnations whistle and spin,
Everyone cheers as fireworks begin.
Wood piled high is eaten by flame,
On top Guy Fawkes gets roasted again,
Rockets return, blackened to ash,
Kaleidoscope colours collide and clash,
Somewhere a screech, and somewhere a crash.

My Teacher

My teacher once wore nappies
My teacher used to crawl
My teacher used to cry at night
My teacher used to bawl.

My teacher jibber jabbered
My teacher ran up stairs
My teacher wrote in squiggles
My teacher stood on chairs.

My teacher once was naughty
My teacher was so rude
My teacher used a bad word
My teacher spilled her food.

My teacher lost her homework
My teacher took too long
My teacher got detention
My teacher did things wrong.

My teacher's all grown-up now
My teacher can't recall
My teacher thinks she's different
My teacher's not at all.

Nobody Likes You
When You Grow Up

Nobody likes you when you grow up.
Nobody offers to steady your cup,
Feeds you food on the end of a fork
Or thinks that you're great for learning to walk.

Nobody holds your hand on the stair
Or whips out a comb to tidy your hair,
Rubs your face to get rid of the dirt,
Kisses you better whenever you're hurt.

Nobody sings you songs in the dark,
Carries you home after games in the park,
Strokes your forehead and tickles your chin,
Praises the width of your mischievous grin.

When things you touch just happen to break,
Nobody says, 'It was just a mistake.
Oh, whoops-a-daisy! We'll pick it up.'
No, nobody likes you when you grow up.

Printed in Great Britain
by Amazon.co.uk, Ltd.,
Marston Gate.